Musli... ...sts

AL - KHAZINI
Founder of Gravity Theory

Published by Ali Gator Productions
Copyright © 2021 Ali Gator Productions, Second Edition,
First Published 2019

National Library of Australia Cataloguing–in-Publication (CIP) data:
Ahmed Imam
ISBN: 978-1-921772-69-6
For primary school age, Juvenile fiction, Dewey Number: 823.92

Adapted from the original title Ilmuan Muslim Ibnu Khazini first published by Pelangi Mizan.
Copyright © 2015 by Author Risma Dewi, Illustrator Nano. Printed in Indonesia.

T: +61 (3) 9386 2771
P.O. Box 2536, Regent West, Melbourne Victoria, 3072 Australia
E: info@ali-gator.com W: www.ali-gator.com

بِسْمِ اللهِ الرَّحْمٰنِ الرَّحِيمِ

BISMILLAHIR RAHMANIR RAHIM

IN THE NAME OF ALLAH, MOST GRACIOUS, MOST MERCIFUL

Inspiring our children to learn about
the great Muslim scientists, scholars
and adventurers from
the Golden Age of Islam.

NOTES TO PARENTS AND TEACHERS

The Muslim Scientists Series aims to introduce to young readers some of the famous Muslim scientists, scholars and adventurers who discovered and invented many things that we use today and take for granted.

It is our hope that young children will be inspired by these amazing people and be encouraged to pursue their own path of discovery and questioning. It all starts with a passion for learning.

Whilst reading about Al-Khazini talk to the children about how they weigh themselves today ?

Ask them if we couldn't weigh things how would this change their life e.g. when they go shopping and buy fruit & vegetables.

Discuss with them about gravity, how everything goes up must come down.

In Sha Allah (God Willing) if this series helps to inspire our young readers to be the next generation of thinkers, to better mankind through inventions and discoveries, then we have truly met our goal.

Abu Al-Fath Abd Al-Rahman
Mansur Al-Khazini or simply
known as Al-Khazini was
a famous scientist
from Seljuk, Persia.

From a young age Al-Khazini studied Literature, Mathematics, Philosophy and Astronomy.

Yet it was mathematics and astronomy that Al-Khazini was really interested in.

Al-Khazini was the first to explain the position of 46 stars.

His understanding of the stars and astronomy was way beyond any other scientists of his time.

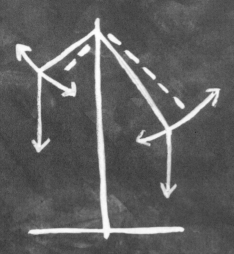

It was his theory on gravity
and weights that made him famous.

He explained scales and weights
and how the temperature
of an object effects its weight.

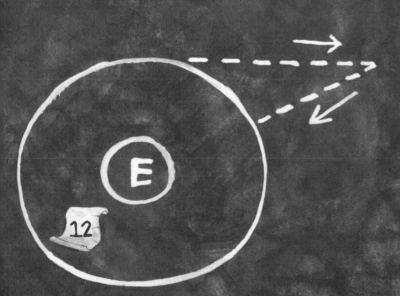

E

12

Al-Khazini's theory on gravity also explained how objects are pulled towards the center of the earth.

His theory is the basis of all mechanical engineering of today.

Al-Khazini built many tools based on
his understanding of gravity, balances and scales.

This lead to the accurate measurement of weights
for the first time.

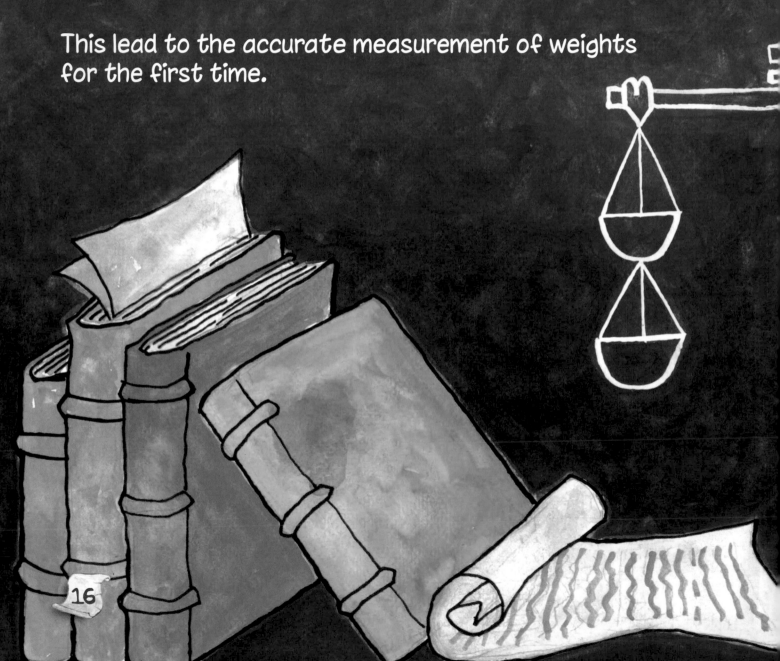

Al-Khazini's theory on gravity was so respected it was used across Europe by other scientists for centuries.

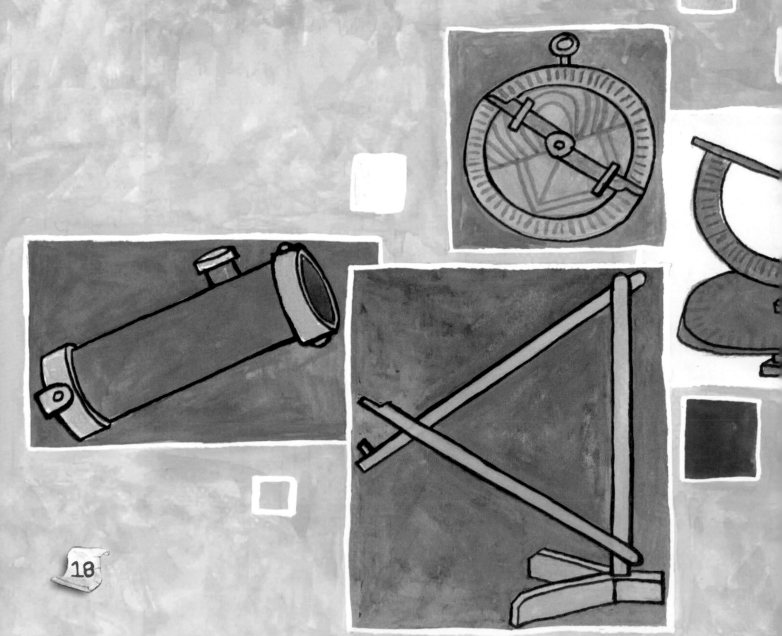

Al-Khazini wrote many books, yet his most famous book is "Mizan Al-Hikmah" (The Balance of Wisdom).

21

There are some examples of gravity on this page, can you name them ?

23

الحَمْدُلله

ALHAMDULILLAH - PRAISE BE TO ALLAH

فَمَنْ ثَقُلَتْ مَوَازِينُهُ فَأُولَٰئِكَ هُمُ الْمُفْلِحُونَ

And those whose scales are heavy
(with good deeds).
It is they who are successful.

Qur'an Surah: 23 (Al-Mu'minun) Verse: 102

24